Special thanks to
Jasmine, Siena, Kim, & Rob

Copyright © 2021 by Scott Erickson
Published in Canada by To the Stars Publishing
ISBN: 978-1-990247-02-6 (hardcover)

Here is a tree in the garden. Every summer it produces apples. We call it an apple tree because the tree "apples."

Here is a tree in the orchard.
Every summer it produces peaches.
We call it a peach tree because
the tree "peaches."

Here is a tree in the jungle. Every year it produces mangoes. We call it a mango tree because the tree "mangoes."

Here is a tree on the beach. Every year it produces coconuts. We call it a coconut tree because the tree "coconuts."

Here is a tree in the desert. Every year it produces dates. We call it a date tree because the tree "dates."

Here is a tree in the forest.
Every summer it produces pine cones.
We call it a pine tree because
the tree "pine cones."

Here is a tree in the grove.
Every year it produces olives.
We call it an olive tree because
the tree "olives."

Here is planet Earth inside our solar system.

Here is the solar system inside our galaxy.

Here is the galaxy
inside our universe.

The planet Earth "peoples" the same way an apple tree "apples." People grow out of the Earth, as the Earth grows out of the solar system, and the solar system grows out of the galaxy, and the galaxy grows out of the universe. Everything grows out of everything. This is how life goes.

Which comes first, the apple tree or the apple?
We cannot say because the apple tree and
the apple are a single process.
The apple grows out of the apple tree.
The apple tree grows out of the apple.
This is how life goes.

Which comes first, the chicken or the egg?
We cannot say because the chicken
and the egg are a single process.
The chicken grows out of the egg.
The egg grows out of the chicken.
This is how life goes.

Which comes first, you or the universe?
We cannot say because you and the
universe are a single process.
You grow out of the universe.
The universe grows out of you.
This is how life goes.